Next Month!
Girls' Basketball

Team Tryouts

Time for the Team

by Edward J. Scarry
illustrated by Kristin Varner

PEARSON

Glenview, Illinois • Boston, Massachusetts • Chandler, Arizona
Upper Saddle River, New Jersey

María is a very busy girl. She studies hard and gets good grades in school. She is on the math team and writes for the school newspaper. She also takes piano lessons. María does not have a lot of free time!

María sees a poster for the girls' basketball team. The team is having a tryout for new players in one month. María loves basketball! But she is so busy! Will she have time to join the team?

---

tryout: a test to see who can join a team

3

"I want to join the basketball team," says María. "The tryouts are in one month. What do you think?"

"That sounds splendid!" says María's father. "But remember you are already very busy. Do you have time?"

"You need time to practice," says María's mother.

María's Schedule
Monday: 3 to 4 P.M. piano lesson
Tuesday: 3 to 5 P.M. math team
         5:30 to 6 P.M. piano practice
Wednesday: 5:30 to 6 P.M. piano practice
Thursday: 3 to 6 P.M. piano practice
Friday: 3 to 5 P.M. math team
Saturday: 9 to 10 A.M. School newspaper
Sunday: 5:30 to 6 P.M. Piano lesson
        Piano practice

María writes her schedule. She wants to see if she has time to practice for the tryouts. "I have time for long practices on Wednesday, Saturday, and Sunday," she tells her parents. "But I will practice on the other days, too."

---

schedule: a list of when someone will do things

5

María practices every day. On Wednesday, Saturday, and Sunday, she practices with her friends or with her father. On the other days, she practices by herself. She works on dribbling and shooting the basketball.

dribbling: bouncing a basketball

The time goes quickly. María feels ready for the tryouts. She has practiced a lot. Now it is time to show what she can do.

"Remember what you learned!" says María's father.

"Good luck!" says María's mother.

María remembers what she practiced. She plays well. She gets a chance to shoot the ball. SWISH. . . the ball goes through the basket!

When the tryouts are over, the coach talks to María.

"Welcome to the team!" she says.

"Thank you, Coach Miller!" says María happily.